EXPLORING WORLD CULTURES

Jamaica

Alicia Z. Klepeis

Cavendish
Square

New York

Published in 2019 by Cavendish Square Publishing, LLC
243 5th Avenue, Suite 136, New York, NY 10016

Website: cavendishsq.com

This publication represents the opinions and views of the author based on his or her personal experience, knowledge, and
research. The information in this book serves as a general guide only. The author and publisher have used their best efforts
in preparing this book and disclaim liability rising directly or indirectly from the use and application of this book.

All websites were available and accurate when this book was sent to press.

Library of Congress Cataloging-in-Publication Data

Names: Klepeis, Alicia, 1971- author.
Title: Jamaica / Alicia Z. Klepeis.
Description: First edition. | New York : Cavendish Square, 2019. | Series:
Exploring world cultures | Includes bibliographical references and index. | Audience: Grades 2-5.
Identifiers: LCCN 2017046638 (print) | LCCN 2017051401 (ebook) | ISBN 9781502638052 (library bound) |
ISBN 9781502639912 (pbk.) | ISBN 9781502639080 (6 pack) | ISBN 9781502639073 (ebook)
Subjects: LCSH: Jamaica--Juvenile literature.
Classification: LCC F1872.2 (ebook) | LCC F1872.2 .K55 2018 (print) | DDC
972.92--dc23
LC record available at https://lccn.loc.gov/2017046638

Editorial Director: David McNamara
Editor: Jodyanne Benson
Copy Editor: Rebecca Rohan
Associate Art Director: Amy Greenan
Designer: Christina Shults
Production Coordinator: Karol Szymczuk
Photo Research: J8 Media

Printed in the United States of America

Contents

Introduction

Jamaica is a North American country in the Caribbean Sea. It has a variety of traditions and celebrations. People have lived in Jamaica for many centuries. Different groups of people have ruled what is now Jamaica. Today, Jamaica is a free country.

People in Jamaica have many kinds of jobs. Some work in hotels, schools, or shops. Others catch fish from the sea or work in mines. Jamaican farmers grow different crops on their land, like sugarcane and bananas.

Jamaica has many beautiful places to visit. There are mountains, waterfalls, and caves. Visitors come from around the world to enjoy Jamaica's beaches and play golf or scuba dive.

Jamaican people value the arts, music, and literature. They are known for reggae music and storytelling. They also enjoy eating spicy food and playing sports.

Jamaica is a fascinating country to explore.

Jamaica has a lot of lovely beaches to enjoy. One popular beach is Montego Bay.

Geography

Jamaica is an island located in the Caribbean Sea. Jamaica is part of North America. It is a little smaller than the state of Connecticut. The country covers 10,991 square miles (28,467 square kilometers). It does not border any other countries.

Jamaica is divided into fourteen parishes.

There are many mountainous areas in Jamaica. Almost half of the island is over 1,000 feet (330 meters) above sea level. Jamaica's Blue Mountains are in the eastern part of the country. The central highland area of Jamaica has underground streams and sinkholes. Sinkholes are large holes in the ground where water collects,

Jamaica's Plants

Jamaica is home to many different plants. Hundreds of varieties of ferns and orchids grow here.

wearing away underground rock. This can cause the ground to collapse.

A red-billed streamertail feeds on a bleeding-heart vine in Montego Bay.

Jamaica has coastal lowlands. They are found in the north and south. These areas have beaches and farms. Many rivers flow in Jamaica, including the Black River and the Rio Minho.

FACT!

Jamaica has a hot and humid climate all year round. However, it is cooler in the mountains.

7

History

People have lived in what is now Jamaica for thousands of years. The first inhabitants are believed to be the Arawak people (also called the Taino). They came to Jamaica from South America around

The Arawak are celebrated as part of Jamaica's history.

2,500 years ago. The Arawak called this island Xaymaca, meaning "land of wood and water." They farmed and fished.

In 1494, explorer Christopher Columbus landed in Jamaica. Columbus and his men fought with the Arawak. Many Arawak died from disease or from being overworked. The Spanish ruled Jamaica until the English took control in 1655.

In 1692, an earthquake destroyed the city of Port Royal. Survivors of the earthquake founded the city of Kingston.

Many slaves were brought over from Africa to work on Jamaica's sugar plantations. Slavery was outlawed in the 1830s. Jamaica remained an English colony until 1962. Today, Jamaica is an independent country.

Sir Alexander Bustamante

Alexander Bustamante was Jamaica's first prime minister after Jamaica gained independence from England. While in office, he worked to build roads, schools, and hospitals on the island.

Bustamante became Jamaica's prime minister in 1962.

Jamaica is a constitutional monarchy. This means that the king or queen does not have complete power. Jamaica also has a **parliament** that makes laws. The capital of Jamaica is the city of Kingston.

This stamp shows Gordon House, where parliament meets.

Jamaica's government has three parts:

- legislative: This part of the government is called the parliament. People in the parliament write new laws.

- judicial: The courts make up this part of Jamaica's government. They follow the country's constitution. It describes the laws of Jamaica.

- executive: The queen of England is the chief of state for Jamaica. The head of government is the prime minister.

Jamaica's parliament is made up of two houses. Its Senate has twenty-one members. Its House of Representatives has sixty-three members. They gather in the George William Gordon House to pass laws.

Women in Jamaica

About 17 percent of the members of Jamaica's parliament are women. However, the Jamaican government has set a goal of having women in 30 percent of its decision-making positions.

Jamaican foreign minister Kamina Johnson Smith

The Economy

Jamaica has one of the smaller economies in North America. However, it trades with countries around the world. Jamaica's most important trading partners include the United States, Canada, and China. Its **currency** is the Jamaican dollar.

Beautiful resorts like this attract many visitors to Jamaica.

About two out of three Jamaican workers have service jobs. Some work in banks, hotels, and restaurants. Others have jobs in shops, hospitals, and museums.

Jamaican workers make many different products. These range from everyday items like clothing and paper to beverages such as rum.

Over two million tourists visited Jamaica from other countries in 2016.

Jamaica is surrounded by water. The nation's fishermen gather food from the sea, both to eat and to sell. In the countryside, farmers grow many crops. Sugarcane, bananas, and yams are a few. Workers called miners dig minerals from below the earth's surface. **Bauxite** is one example.

A power shovel loads bauxite at a mine.

Jamaican Coffee

Jamaica is known for the excellent quality of its coffee. The country's Blue Mountain Coffee sells for high prices around the world.

The Environment

Jamaica's people, plants, and animals need clean air and water to live. However, some places in Jamaica do not have these things.

Smog in Kingston blocks the view of the landscape.

Air pollution is a problem in parts of Jamaica. The two main sources of this pollution are cars and industrial activities. Making cement and processing bauxite cause pollution. As more people get cars, the air in cities like Kingston gets dirtier.

Water pollution is also a problem in Jamaica. Oil spills and industrial waste threaten the water quality here. Pollution can damage the coral

FACT!

The Jamaican rock iguana is one of several endangered animals living in Jamaica. It is one of the rarest lizards on Earth.

reefs along Jamaica's coast. Overfishing and hurricanes also threaten these coral reefs.

Much of Jamaica's original forest has been cut down. People cut trees down mainly for agriculture but also for new buildings and tourism sites.

A Jamaican iguana suns itself on a tree branch.

Clean Energy in Jamaica

Jamaica is working to get more of its electricity from clean sources. One example of a clean energy source is solar power. Solar power uses the sun's energy.

15

Nearly three million people live in Jamaica. The country's national motto is "Out of Many, One People." Jamaicans belong to a variety of ethnic backgrounds and cultures.

This young boy is wearing his school uniform in Falmouth, Jamaica.

More than nine out of ten people here are of African descent. The ancestors of many black Jamaicans came from West Africa. Over 6 percent of Jamaicans are people of mixed heritage.

Almost 1 percent of Jamaica's people are East Indian. Many of their ancestors came to Jamaica

FACT!

Jamaica's biggest city is Kingston. It is home to over 580,000 people.

from India. Today most East Indian Jamaicans live in the nation's cities, like Kingston.

Jamaica is also home to several smaller groups of people. The country has communities of German, Chinese, and Middle Eastern people. All of these groups brought their own cultures and traditions to Jamaica.

Jamaicans Abroad

Almost three million Jamaicans live outside of the island in other countries. Many of these people work and send money back home to help their families.

Lifestyle

People in Jamaica live in many different places. Nearly 55 percent of Jamaicans live in cities and towns. Some live in apartments. Others live in houses. Kingston also has areas where housing conditions are poor.

This house is part of the poorer area of Kingston.

People in the city might walk, ride a bike, or take a bus to work. Families here often have cell phones and televisions. Unfortunately, crime is a big problem in some neighborhoods.

People living in the Jamaican countryside often lead slower-paced lives. Some grow crops to sell. Others grow food to feed their families.

On average, most Jamaican women have two children.

Jamaicans in the rural areas may work as miners. Some have jobs at resorts or in national parks.

Many Jamaican women today have jobs outside of the home. They work as businesspeople, lawyers, and engineers.

This Jamaican woman works in medicine.

Extended Families

In Jamaica, it is common for children, parents, and grandparents to live together. Grandmothers often will take care of their preschool-age grandchildren while their parents are at work.

19

Religion

Jamaica has no official religion. People can believe what they want to believe. Religion is important to many Jamaican people. More than two out of three people here are Christian. There are also smaller groups of Roman Catholics and Jehovah's Witnesses.

These Jamaicans are at a Catholic service.

Christian church services are held every Sunday in cities and villages throughout Jamaica.

FACT!

More than 21 percent of Jamaica's people do not follow any religion at all.

These services usually involve music. As in other nations, Jamaican Christians celebrate certain holidays, like Christmas and Easter.

In addition to Christians, Jamaica is also home to small Hindu and Buddhist populations. There are also Muslims. Jamaica's Jewish community has a long history.

This photo shows a Rastafarian man in Negril, Jamaica.

Rastafarianism

A small percent of Jamaicans follows a religion called Rastafarianism. People who follow this religion believe Ethiopian emperor Haile Selassie I is God. They follow rules about foods, such as not eating pork or not drinking milk or coffee.

Language

English is the official language of Jamaica. The country's government uses English. People speak English for business matters. In school, children are also taught in English.

Newspapers, such as the *Jamaican Observer*, are written in English.

Jamaican English sounds different from the English people speak in the United States. Most Jamaicans speak English patois (PA-twa). Patois is the dialect spoken by a particular group.

In 2016, a woman from London created a doll named Toya that speaks Jamaican patois. The doll has become a popular item around the world.

English patois is a local dialect developed as African slaves in Jamaica communicated with their English-speaking masters. Jamaican patois has its own vocabulary and grammar.

In addition to English and patois, some Jamaicans also speak other languages. For example, **immigrants** who have come to Jamaica from different places may speak languages other than English. Chinese is just one example.

Some people in Jamaica learn to speak more than one language. Schools here commonly teach children French and Spanish.

Arts and Festivals

People throughout Jamaica enjoy the arts. Cave paintings made by the Taino people are the island's earliest artworks. Modern-day artists liven up even the nation's poorest neighborhoods by making colorful murals.

Dancers perform in Falmouth for tourists.

Dance is another important part of Jamaican culture. The *mento* is a traditional dance performed here. But mento also refers to a type of Jamaican folk music. It features bongo drums and the **rhumba box**.

Around the world, Jamaica is known for reggae music. The electric guitar and the organ are important instruments in reggae music.

One of Jamaica's most celebrated poets is Louise Bennett. Her poems are about everyday life. They are often performed aloud.

Jamaica has festivals throughout the year. Jamaicans celebrate Independence Day on August 6. This national holiday celebrates the country gaining its independence from the United Kingdom.

Bob Marley

Kingston is home to the Bob Marley Museum. Bob Marley is probably the world's most famous reggae musician. The museum is on the site of Marley's home where he lived until his death in 1981.

Fun and Play

There are many ways to have fun in Jamaica. Lots of Jamaican people enjoy sports. Soccer is a popular sport here. Many people also play cricket. Cricket is similar to baseball. It is played with a bat and ball. Basketball and track and field are also well-liked in Jamaica.

A group of Rastafarian men play checkers at a local community center.

FACT!

Tubing on Jamaica's rivers is a fun activity. The White River and the Rio Bueno are two great spots for tubing.

In their free time, many Jamaicans enjoy spending time at the beach. People often swim and fish. Water activities like scuba diving and snorkeling are also popular with local people and tourists visiting Jamaica.

Many Jamaicans like to play games. Dominoes are quite popular both with school children and adults. Checkers and chess are also commonly played here.

Usain Bolt is running to the finish line.

"The Fastest Man Alive"

Usain Bolt is probably the most famous athlete from Jamaica. He is their biggest track and field star. He has won many Olympic gold medals for his sprinting.

Food

People in Jamaica eat many different kinds of food. Jamaican cooks use a variety of spices in their dishes. Pimento (also known as allspice) and curry powder are popular spices here.

Jerk chicken is cooking on a barbeque.

Seafood is often eaten in Jamaican homes and restaurants. The country's national dish is **ackee** and saltfish. Some cooks serve this dish with fried flour dumplings. Others offer it alongside boiled bananas.

FACT!

Bammy is a common breakfast dish in Jamaica. It's a flatbread made from grated **cassava.**

People in Jamaica also enjoy stews and jerked meat. Cooks spice up pork, chicken, or fish with jerk seasoning before barbecuing it. This seasoning contains a mixture of hot peppers, pimento, lime juice, and other spices.

Jamaicans have access to lots of different fruits, such as bananas, pineapples, and papayas. Juice, coffee, and rum are popular beverages here.

Fruits like melon and papaya are popular in Jamaica.

Jamaican Ice Cream

Jamaican ice cream flavors go way beyond vanilla. Folks here can enjoy scoops of ginger, passion fruit, mango, rum and raisin, or even grape nut ice cream.

Glossary

ackee   A tropical red fruit that grows across Jamaica.

bauxite   A claylike rock that makes up aluminum.

cassava   The starchy root of a tropical tree used as food.

currency   Money, such as that being used in a country or region.

immigrants   People who have moved into a foreign country to live there.

parliament   The group of people in government responsible for making laws.

rhumba box   A square musical instrument that has strings; a kind of large thumb piano.

Find Out More

Books

Capek, Michael. *Jamaica.* Country Explorers.
Minneapolis, MN: Lerner Publishing Group,
Inc., 2010.

Owings, Lisa. *Jamaica.* Exploring Countries.
Minneapolis, MN: Bellwether Media, 2014.

Website

National Geographic Kids: Jamaica

http://kids.nationalgeographic.com/explore
countries/jamaica/#jamaica-beach.jpg

Video

Lonely Planet: Introducing Jamaica

https://www.lonelyplanet.com/video/introducing-
jamaica/v/vid/76

Index

About the Author

Alicia Z. Klepeis began her career at the National Geographic Society. She is the author of many children's books, including *Haunted Cemeteries Around the World*, *Bizarre Things We've Called Medicine*, and *A Time For Change*. She lives with her family in upstate New York.